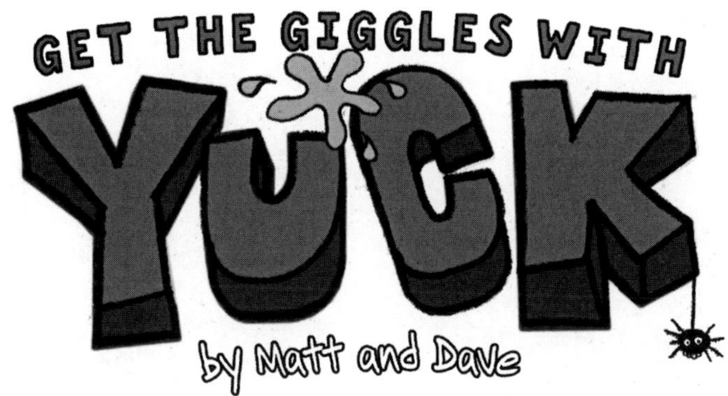

Yuck's Slobbery Dog

Illustrated by Nigel Baines

Chapters | Page

1
The Slobbery Dog

Yuck was walking home from school with his sister Polly Princess, when a dog started following them. It was slobbering and it licked Polly's hand.

"**UUURGH!**" she yelled.

Yuck giggled.

“What a horrible, slobbery dog,” Polly said. The dog was brown and dirty and smelly. “Go away!”

But the dog just wagged its tail.

Yuck bent down and gave it a stroke. “It’s only being friendly,” he said.

The dog had a collar with a tag on, but there was no sign of its owner.

“Are you lost?” Yuck asked it. “Do you need someone to look after you?”

“Woof,” the dog barked.

Yuck checked the metal tag on the dog's collar and read its name: Scruff.

"Come on. Leave it alone, Yuck," Polly called, crossing the street.

But as Yuck followed her, Scruff followed, too. In fact, the dog followed them all the way home. Then, when Yuck went indoors, Scruff ran in after him. He bounded upstairs to Yuck's room.

Scruff licked Yuck's face and Yuck laughed.

Scruff held out his paw for Yuck to shake.

"You're not horrible," Yuck said. "You're a clever dog."

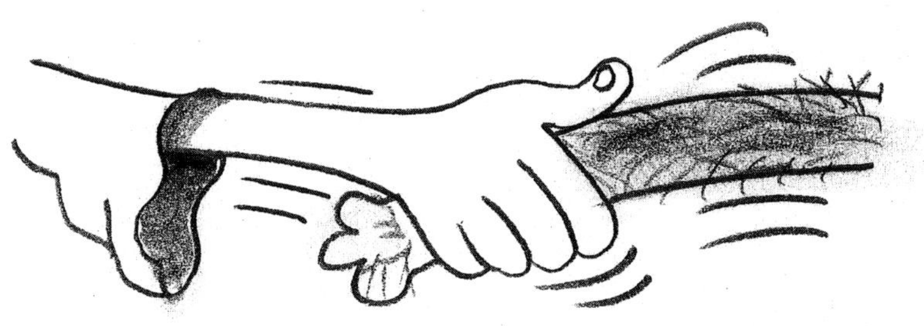

"Can you sit?" Yuck asked.

Scruff sat up straight.

"Can you roll over?"

Scruff rolled over on the carpet and Yuck tickled his tummy. Scruff could do tricks!

"I think you're the best dog in the world," Yuck said. "If you were my dog, I'd teach you lots of tricks."

Yuck imagined teaching Scruff how to jump through a hoop, then how to ride a motorbike.

Scruff would be famous! Crowds would cheer as Scruff flew through the hoop on his motorbike, juggling sausages!

2
Out in the Cold

"It's dinner time, Yuck!" Mum called from downstairs.

Yuck sneaked the dog into the kitchen where Mum, Dad and Polly were having dinner. Yuck sat down and Scruff crept under the table. Yuck slipped a sausage from his plate and Scruff gobbled it up.

Scruff slobbered on Polly's shoe.

"**UUURGH!**" Polly said. She looked under the table. "It's that revolting slobbery dog!"

Mum and Dad bent down to see.

"What on earth is a dog doing in here?" Mum asked.

“It followed us home,” Yuck told her. “It needs looking after.”

“It’s smelly and revolting,” Polly said.

Mum opened the back door. “I’m afraid it’ll have to stay in the garden, Yuck.”

“But Mum ...”

“It’s dirty, Yuck.”

Scruff looked up at Yuck with big, brown eyes.

Yuck watched as the dog walked sadly out.

“I hope it runs away,” Polly said, sticking her tongue out.

Yuck decided that when he was **EMPEROR OF EVERYTHING** he'd have lots of slobbery dogs. They would all live indoors and woof and play in a big Doggie Doo Dah band. Anyone who was mean to dogs would be thrown into the **SEA OF SLOBBER**.

3
Scruff's Scratchy Surprise

Later that evening, Yuck looked out of his bedroom window. It was getting dark outside and it was raining, too. He could see Scruff sitting on the lawn, shivering. Poor Scruff, he thought.

The dog began to howl. It's not fair, Yuck thought. Just because Scruff's dirty and smelly, there's no need to be nasty to him.

While Mum, Dad and Polly were watching television, Yuck secretly let Scruff back in and led him upstairs.

Yuck lay on his bed with Scruff beside him, snuggled in Yuck's blanket.

Scruff was wet and muddy. He was scratching with his back leg. Yuck could see fleas hopping in the dog's fur. He had an idea.

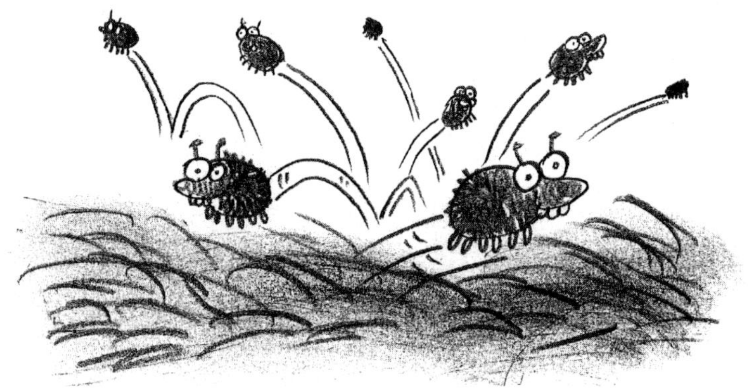

Yuck picked the fleas off and put them in a jam jar. Then, that night, while Polly was asleep, he crept into her room.

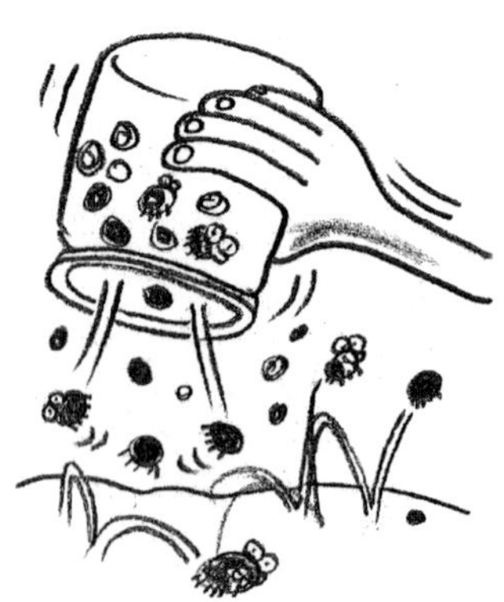

He lifted her blanket and tipped the fleas into her bed.

That'll teach her to be mean to Scruff, he thought.

The next morning, Yuck took Scruff for a walk around the garden and Scruff jumped in the puddles.

As Yuck was sneaking Scruff back upstairs, he heard a scream from Polly's room. He ran to her door. "What's the matter?" he asked.

Polly was in her pyjamas, scratching.

"I'm covered in fleas!" she yelled.

Yuck giggled.

Then Scruff ran in wagging his tail.

"Hey, what's that disgusting dog doing in the house?" Polly said. "He's given me fleas!"

"But Scruff's a nice dog," Yuck said. "Scruff, go and give Polly a kiss."

Scruff jumped up and licked Polly's face.

"**UUURGH**, that's disgusting!" Polly screamed, dog spit splattering her mouth.

"He's just being friendly," Yuck said.

Polly pushed Scruff off. She saw muddy paw prints on her carpet.

"He's filthy, Yuck!"

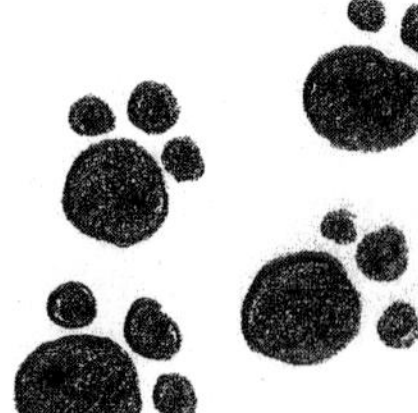

Scruff shook his fur, sending mud all over Polly's bedroom.

"Mum!" Polly shouted, running downstairs. "Yuck's got that dog in the house again!"

"Quick, hide!" Yuck said to Scruff. He lifted Polly's blanket and Scruff dived under it.

Mum burst in and saw the paw prints and mud. "Yuck, where's that dog?" she asked.

"He's not in here," Yuck said.

Polly came in. "Yes he is. I can smell him."

Just then, a wagging tail poked out from under Polly's blanket.

Mum pulled the blanket off and Scruff stood up and barked.

"Woof!"

"POO!" Polly screamed. In the middle of her bed sheet was a curly lump of dog poo. "THAT DOG'S POOED IN MY BED!"

"THAT'S REVOLTING!" Mum said.

"Yuck, that dog is **NEVER** to come indoors again!" Mum said. She dragged Scruff back into the garden.

"Yuck, go and clean Polly's room," Mum said, handing him a sponge and a bowl of soapy water.

4
Plotting Polly

While Yuck cleaned the mess in Polly's room, Polly headed downstairs.

"Mum, I think I'll take Scruff for a walk," she said.

"Really, Polly? I thought you didn't like that dog," Mum replied.

Polly grinned, then stepped out of the back door.

"Walkies, Scruff!"

Scruff began wagging his tail.

Polly clipped Scruff's lead on. He pulled her out of the gate and through the town to the park.

"You're a horrible dog," she said. "Now it's time to get rid of you for good."

Polly unclipped Scruff's lead then threw a stick as far as she could.

"Fetch!" she said.

As Scruff raced to fetch the stick, Polly climbed a tree and hid amongst its branches. She sniggered as Scruff came back to find her with the stick in his mouth. He was looking for Polly, but she stayed hidden.

"Stupid slobbery dog," Polly muttered. She grinned as Scruff wandered off looking for her.

Polly climbed down from the tree. "Good riddance," she said, sneaking back out of the park.

5
The Best Dog in the World

When Polly arrived home, Yuck was at the back door calling for Scruff.

"Scruff's gone," Polly told him, grinning. "I took him to the park and he ran away."

"Ran away?" Yuck asked. "You did something to him, didn't you?"

"It serves that dog right for messing up my room," Polly said.

Yuck raced off as fast as he could.

"Where are you going?" Polly called.

"To find Scruff!" Yuck said.

Yuck raced through the town and into the park. "Here, Scruff!" he called. But there was no sign of the dog anywhere.

Yuck ran past the swings. **"Scruff!"**

He ran around the pond. **"Scruff!"**

Then he ran past an old lady. **"Scruff!"**

"Did you say Scruff?" the old lady asked.

The old lady was pinning a piece of paper to a tree. It was a picture of Scruff. Above it she'd written: **LOST DOG.** Below it she'd written: **REWARD.**

"You must be Scruff's owner," Yuck said.

Just then, he heard a "**Woof!**" He saw Scruff sprinting from the bushes.

The dog jumped up and licked Yuck's face. "We've found you!" Yuck said.

Then Scruff jumped up to the old lady and licked her face, too.

"Oh, Scruff, I'm so pleased you're OK," she said.

"I've been looking after him," Yuck told her.

"Woof!" Scruff barked, wagging his tail.

Scruff shook Yuck's hand, then sat up, then rolled over.

"He's a very clever dog," Yuck said.

“He’s the best dog in the world,” the lady replied. She reached into her coat pocket and took out a ten dollar note. “Here you are,” she said, handing the money to Yuck.

“Ten dollars! For me?” Yuck asked.

“It’s the reward for finding Scruff,” the old lady said.

Yuck smiled and gave Scruff a great big hug. “He was no trouble at all.”

When Yuck got home, Polly was in the kitchen with Mum.

"Ha!" Polly said, seeing Yuck arrive without Scruff. "So you didn't find that dog, then?"

"Yes I did," Yuck told her. "No thanks to you."

"What do you mean, Yuck?" Mum asked.

"Polly took Scruff to the park just so she could get rid of him," Yuck explained.

"Is that true, Polly?" Mum asked.

"That dog was revolting," Polly replied. She was scratching herself all over.

Mum frowned at her. "Even so, no dog deserves to be abandoned."

"It's OK, Mum, I found his owner too," Yuck said.

"His owner?" Polly asked.

"She was a very nice lady," Yuck replied. "She even gave me a reward."

Yuck took the ten dollar note from his pocket and showed it to Polly and Mum.

"That's not fair!" Polly said. "I want a reward!"

"There'll be no reward for you, Polly," Mum said. "And as punishment for leaving Scruff in the park, there'll be no pocket money for a whole month, either."

"But, Mum ..."

"No buts," Mum told her.

Yuck giggled. "Don't worry, Polly. At least you got something. You got fleas!"